D0393895

Praise for *7 Tenets of Taxi Terry*

"*The 7 Tenets of Taxi Terry* may just save our sanity and common sense through Scott McKain's distinctive and positive approach to business–and life itself."
—Joe Bonsall, forty-year member of the legendary music group, The Oak Ridge Boys, and author of the bestselling book *G.I. Joe and Lillie.*

"Scott McKain's latest book, *The 7 Tenets of Taxi Terry,* is a must-read for any professional or organization attempting to creatively differentiate itself from the competition."
—Don Hutson, coauthor of the #1 *New York Times* bestseller *The One-Minute Entrepreneur* and CEO of U. S. Learning

"As the marketplace becomes more commoditized and impersonal, the more important it becomes to differentiate with customer experience that can't be copied. No one understands the art and science of customer experience better than Scott McKain. Every leader, manager, and employee in your company should read this book now!"
—Joe Calloway, bestselling author of *Be the Best at What Matters Most* and Hall of Fame professional speaker

"An 'ultimate customer experience' is not an option in business. In a world where the word 'commodity' has become the norm, Scott McKain clarifies the all-important (and all-profitable) strategy to become *different,* become *distinct,* and become *dominant* in your marketplace. Buy this book. Read it. And put it into practice."
—Jeffrey Gitomer, author of *The Little Red Book of Selling*

"Scott McKain is a great storyteller and *Taxi Terry* delivers: it provides you what you need to know and do to provide your customers with the kind of experience that will delight them and keep them coming back for more."
—Mark Sanborn, author of *The Fred Factor* and CEO of Sanborn and Associates

"In *The 7 Tenets of Taxi Terry* Scott McKain clearly shows again why he is the master at teaching companies how they can out-market, out-sell and out-service their competition."
—Dr. Tony Alessandra, author of *The Platinum Rule* and *The NEW Art of Managing People*

"If a taxi driver can turn an everyday ride into an extraordinary experience, what's your excuse? Do your customers love you enough to sell for you? If not, there's work to be done because Taxi Terry's customers sell for him every day. Scott McKain shows you how to consistently deliver a level of service that makes you and your business distinctive in the hearts and minds of your customers with this practical and engaging book. You will want every person in your company to read this book and apply its lessons."
—Randy G. Pennington, author of the award-winning bestseller *Make Change Work*

"The unique perspectives revealed in *The 7 Tenets of Taxi Terry* are lessons that can be adapted to any business of any size. This book is another masterpiece from the brilliant business mind of Scott McKain."
—Patricia Fripp, CSP, CPAE, former president of the National Speakers Association; one of America's leading executive speech coaches

"I have loved the story of *Taxi Terry* every time I've heard Scott tell it. It's entertaining, funny, and always a crowd pleaser, as well over 100,000 YouTube viewers will attest. But there is so much more to the story. Finally, in this great book, Scott gives you a chance to go deeper into the story and learn the lessons you need to deliver a great customer service experience."
—Larry Winget, television personality and six-time bestselling author of *Grow a Pair* and *Shut Up, Stop Whining, and Get a Life!*

How Every Employee Can
Create and Deliver the
Ultimate Customer Experience

7 TENETS OF TAXI TERRY

SCOTT McKAIN

New York   Chicago   San Francisco   Athens   London   Madrid
Mexico City   Milan   New Delhi   Singapore   Sydney   Toronto

1 2 3 4 5 6 7 8 9 0   DOC/DOC   1 2 0 9 8 7 6 5 4

ISBN: 978-0-07-182215-2
MHID: 0-07-182215-1

e-ISBN: 978-0-07-182221-3
e-MHID: 0-07-182221-6

Library of Congress Cataloging-in-Publication Data
McKain, Scott.
  7 tenets of Taxi Terry : how every employee can create and deliver the ultimate customer experience / by Scott McKain.
    pages cm
  ISBN 978-0-07-182215-2 (alk. paper) -- ISBN 0-07-182215-1 (alk. paper)
1. Customer relations. 2. Customer services. I. Title. II. Title: Seven tenets of Taxi Terry.
  HF5415.5.M3827 2014
  658.8'12--dc23
                            2014013239

McGraw-Hill Education books are available at special quantity discounts to use as premiums and sales promotions, or for use in corporate training programs. To contact a representative, please visit the Contact Us page at www.mhprofessional.com.

Although all of my previous books have been inscribed by name to a few specific individuals who made major contributions to and had enormous impacts on my life, this work is simply, sincerely, and quite rightly dedicated to everyone who works hard every day.

From my father who ran a grocery store and drove a truck when I was growing up to my uncles who climbed poles in blizzards so that the lights would stay on for the community, from the single mother cleaning hotel rooms or waiting tables somewhere to the woman juggling difficult schedules and demanding personalities in an office, from the financial advisor helping clients plan for their future to the bank teller dealing with every type of person all day long and from others I've been blessed to encounter in my travels, this book is dedicated to all individuals who bring a passion to their life and the way they make a living.

There is a glorious grandeur when a basic task such as driving a taxicab is done in an extraordinary manner. This book is not intended just to show you how to attain that standard for your organization or, even more important, for yourself. It is also written to celebrate the unforgettable individuals who are teaching these profound lessons in a simple style through the way they work and by the way they live.

Scott McKain
Henderson, Nevada
May 5, 2014

Are you ready for the best business book on the customer experience you've read in your life?

(You'll understand why this is here very soon.)

CONTENTS

INTRODUCTION

"I'm just a _____."

Whether on a personal errand or at a professional engagement, it seems that whenever I ask someone, "What do you do?" the answer tends to be, "Well, I'm just a . . . ," followed by the title of his or her job. That response has always bothered me intensely for two critical reasons.

First, what you do isn't what you are.

Personally, I may be an author and a professional speaker, but I'm also a husband and a stepfather. Depending on when you ask me, I'm also a golfer and a guy who likes to do a lot of other fun stuff. There's a difference between *do* and *are*.

Sometimes people confuse the two, usually to their detriment. I don't want us starting our experience together in this book with you wondering if I understand that being a taxi driver, for example, doesn't mean that is what you *are*. I understand that it is *the activity you perform* as a job. It's your profession.

However, I also believe that the way you approach what you do for a job—the *do*—can affect the type of person you become—the *are*—and we'll discuss that in greater depth later in this book.

It's the second aspect that really rankles me, though. In the vast majority of cases, a person describing what he or she does adds a modifier to the response. Instead of saying, "I'm a bank teller," the answer is, "I'm *only* a bank teller." Many times the retort isn't, "I'm an insurance professional" but is expressed as "I'm *just* an insurance agent." For some reason, many of us feel that we have to disparage—or at least trivialize a bit—our careers. This is especially the case if we find ourselves in a profession or position that we don't believe others find unusual or remarkable.

It's hard to imagine a political figure saying, "I'm *just* our country's representative to the United Nations." A famous driver might exclaim, "I just won the Indianapolis 500." However, he or she definitely would not proclaim, "I'm *just* the winner of the world's most famous race" unless it was a comment meant to be understood as sarcastic.

Let's face it: most of us won't be guzzling milk in Victory Lane or debating diplomats about a sensitive geopolitical crisis in Manhattan. Yet why do so many feel this extraordinary need to downplay something they spend so much time doing?

When I was a child, part of the way in which I learned about how government works (or at least is supposed to operate) was from a simple cartoon shown on a program called *Schoolhouse Rock*. The success of those little videos with their songs and characters continues to this day. The Arlington Heights, IL, *Daily Herald* reports[1] that a cast that is "82 members strong, ranging in age from 7 to 15 and hailing from 15 surrounding communities" has created a live production of *Schoolhouse Rock* and currently performs at a local theater to bring learning home to students in that area.

CNN told the story of the musician Bob Dorough, the originator of *Schoolhouse Rock*.[2] He "was approached in 1971 by a New York advertising executive whose sons were having great difficulty in math class. He asked him to set the multiplication tables to music." Now, 40 years later, those songs still resonate with the baby boomers they educated as well as the Generation Xers and Yers and millennials who have watched them over 30 million times on YouTube. More than 1,000 people recently jammed into the Kennedy Center in Washington, DC, to hear Dorough perform—and to sing along with him—his famed *Schoolhouse Rock* songs.

Remember the one about how a bill becomes a law?

The character wasn't a "bill"; he was "*JUST* a bill . . . on Capitol Hill." In fact, in the song we all memorized, he didn't (and wouldn't) view himself as being important until the president signed him and he then became a "law."

Don't misunderstand me here: I'm not implying that our frequent self-esteem challenges as they relate to our respective jobs are somehow rooted in a four-decade-old song about legislation.

What I am asking you to consider is that just as our friend the "Bill" felt, we often fail to consider what we do as truly valuable. Or we want to defer to someone else's approval (such as "Bill" needing the president's signature) or we require a change in our position (from a "Bill" to a "Law") to reach a point of usefulness. Therefore, we are *"just* a . . . whatever" until an external action or some other individual or group confers on us a higher level of achievement.

That's a significant problem.

The world needs extraordinary taxi drivers and bank tellers. We have enough "just" cabbies and clerks. We are lusting for passionate sales professionals and customer service representatives. We already have plenty of order takers and operators.

The reason for this book is to illuminate for you the seven tenets of creating Ultimate Customer Experiences for the customers and prospects you deal with every single day.

By the way, you'll see the phrase with capital letters—the Ultimate Customer Experience—because that term is a federally registered trademark owned by my company. We have a specific and strategic approach regarding how you and your organization can deliver that type of experience to your customers, and you'll learn a few of those steps on our journey through this book.

However, at this point you may be asking:

- *What if the only reason I have this book is that the company or my boss gave it to me?*

If your company presented you with this book, it says some very positive things about them!

First, it means that they are committed to improving the experiences you create for your customers and colleagues. No organization or individual would invest in an activity in which it had little interest.

You wouldn't buy season tickets to the games of a sports team you didn't care about. You wouldn't watch every episode of a television show you didn't enjoy. Your company would not have given you this book if it was not focused on your important role in enhancing the customer experience.

It also says they are interested in *you*. (Remember, you don't invest in something you aren't interested in.) Your company recognizes that you are its most important asset.

- *What if I, on my own initiative, am investing the time to read this book?*

Well, it obviously means you have initiative in taking the most important step any of us can ever take: the step toward personal growth. You don't acquire and read a book if all you want to do is keep treading water and maintain the status quo. You are making this effort because you have decided to improve yourself personally and professionally.

- *But what if the people I work with do not have the same dedication to internal and external customers that I do?*

Honestly, that's a tough one. It's so much easier to create Ultimate Customer Experiences when the commitment runs throughout the organization. However—and this is a very important point—you have to take personal responsibility for the way you engage the internal or external customers with whom you have contact.

Think about it. I've received great service from companies that I know don't give a darn about my business. You have, too, I'll wager. How did that happen?

There is only one possible answer: an *individual* cared more about you and overcame the obvious deficiencies in his or her colleagues' approach to dealing with customers.

Design your own personal program of growth and development. Listen to audio programs, sign up for online learning, and create your own PhD in achievement. It will make you more valuable wherever your career takes you, whatever you decide to do.

There will be times when you may question whether it is worth it to go the extra mile to serve customers if you aren't receiving the support you deserve.

This can create enormous difficulties for customers. Too many people seem to be behaving as if they believed that if the confirmation of their personal importance fails to come from above in the organization, they will extract it from below. A slang term used in the United States is *mall cop syndrome*; it is employed to criticize people who use the authority of their position to hide behind "company policy" or "corporate procedures" to make things tougher on the very people they should be serving: customers. In some cases, for some people, the top level doesn't make us feel important, so we take it out on our colleagues or our customers and show them that we are the gatekeepers, totally in charge of their customer experience.

You are better than that.

That's why you're reading this book, why it is important to learn the seven tenets inspired by Taxi Terry—who, through the power of the experience he created for me on a simple cab ride, sparked a story that I will relate in the next chapter—and why you are making the commitment to create and deliver the Ultimate Customer Experience.

I will let you in on a secret: there is very little in this book that you will find new or exclusively original. There are no groundbreaking or revolutionary philosophies and no business school theories or high-level management concepts for you to consider. If you've read any of my previous books or my blog, you will come across some ideas and concepts you've already seen; this, of course, is natural because these are the principles about which I am very passionate.

This is a book intended for all of us, from the management team to frontline employees, from executives to executive assistants. It was written to remind each of us of some basic steps we already know but often fail to consistently execute, steps that enable us to connect with the very people who determine our success and our future: customers.

You may think of customers and visualize only those outside the organization who purchase your products and services. However, what if you don't deal directly with external customers?

One of the most important concepts for you to integrate in your efforts is that of internal customers. Popularized in the 1950s by the Romanian-born management consultant Dr. Joseph Juran, it still has great relevance today.

The Elsmar Cove Forum describes it this way[3]: "A simple definition of an internal customer is anyone within an organization who at any time is dependent on anyone else within the organization."

It will help if you develop categories so that you can list all the internal customers you serve and their individual requirements and needs. In addition, you should make a list of the departments and individuals within your organization who are serving you, the places where you are the internal customer.

This is important, because it means that if your boss fails to provide the information or training you need to do your job, he or she has failed you, the internal customer. Therefore, internal customers consist of *everyone* up and down the line within the organization who would be affected if you failed to do your job.

Just as with external customers, internal customers seek, desire, and deserve an Ultimate Customer Experience.

As we discuss the seven tenets in this book, most of the examples will revolve around external customers. However, if your role is exclusively serving internal ones, the steps toward creating the Ultimate Customer Experience are practically identical.

You may be thinking, how can I learn anything that applies to my business from a taxi driver, given the complexity of the industry in which I work? That's a great question.

It's completely possible that you work for an innovative leader in technology or own the local dry cleaners. Perhaps you are a part of a global automotive behemoth, or you could be building your direct-marketing business by selling nutritional products. I understand that there is great variation among the professionals who make up the potential audience of readers for the book you are about to read.

Vast differences will be found in the complexity of the following elements:

- Product

- Selling process

- Technology

- Organizational structure

- Customer

That is just to name a few. One might be selling sophisticated networking hubs for communication platforms, whereas someone else wants to market more T-shirts; some may be serving customers who are larger corporations, whereas others are retail stores; some of you work for companies with thousands of employees, and others are self-employed and working from a home office.

Regardless of where you work or what you do, the fundamental tenets of Taxi Terry are critical for your success. Here are two vital keys to your success:

1. Learn the tenet and understand the guiding principles behind it.

2. Adapt the tenet to your specific situation and adopt it as a practice in your work.

The important point to remember is that you, regardless of your position within the organization, can become an even more influential professional and can do so in your current job, right where you are, right now.

You can enjoy your work more than you currently do. You can earn more money for yourself and deliver more profit to your organization. Perhaps most important, you can have a powerful impact on the customers you serve and the people with whom you work, and you can become an extraordinary example for the lives of those you love and seek to inspire in your personal life.

How do I know you can do this? There are two primary reasons.

First, let me share the experience of my father. He didn't grow up in the greatest circumstances; he was raised in a family with 11 other siblings during a time of great financial hardship. He was a truck driver, butcher, and small-town grocery store owner in his career, yet I never heard Dad say he was, for example, "*just* a meat cutter" at any time. His approach, dedication, and passion continue to inspire everything I do in my life and work.

However, I do not want to give you the impression as we begin our journey in this book that I'm one of those "only do what you love for work" or "make a living at your passion" authors. I do believe your job and your life become easier if you love what you do; however, I also firmly believe that this approach has been incorrectly and inaccurately advised to an astounding degree.

I absolutely love the Indianapolis Colts. When they are playing a game, the world shuts down for me and everything revolves around what they're doing on the football field. I'm fanatical about their games and revel in their success as one of their supporters. I am passionate about the Colts; however, regardless of my degree of fervor, I will never, ever be a member of the team and make my living playing the game along with them.

You see, passion isn't the sole requirement for successful execution of the responsibilities of a job. There are others that are just as critical.

It's akin to those folks who read the book *The Secret* and learn about what they term the law of attraction. Then those readers sit on their tails, thinking intensely about becoming wealthy and hoping to attract riches into their lives. It never—yes, I mean *never*—works.

Think about it: even those who have been the most fortunate in attaining wealth—such as the winners of the multistate lottery game known as Powerball—had to get up, go out, and purchase a ticket for the game. It's not as if they were reclining at home, no Quick Picks in hand, and someone knocked on the door and handed them $200 million.

Passion without effort equals *failure*.

In addition to the element of passion, there is another aspect you should consider.

One of the most fortunate circumstances in my past occurred during my teenage years, when I worked at the local radio station in a nearby town: WMPI radio in Scottsburg, Indiana. A high school friend of the station's manager was a member of a gospel quartet that was singing in various high school auditoriums and churches around the country. On multiple occasions my boss booked his friend's group to play concerts for our station, and I was asked to emcee. The group was known then—and now—as the Oak Ridge Boys.

William Lee Golden—childhood buddy of my boss—became my friend as well and remains so to this day. And I am honored that I can count the other Oak Ridge Boys—Duane Allen, Joe Bonsall, and Richard Sterban, as well as their road manager, Darrick Kinslow—among my closest compadres.

Even now, when I go see the Oak Ridge Boys perform in concert, I am still thrilled by the passion that they continue to bring to their music four decades after that first concert of theirs that I had the pleasure of attending. However, the last thing I would want to see, especially from longtime friends of mine, would be passionate performers who could not carry a tune.

The Oaks are damn fine singers—individually and collectively. They continue to sound fantastic—and they had better continue to do that if they want to continue to pack concert halls around the world.

Regardless of their passion, the Oak Ridge Boys must deliver a significant degree of performing skill at their concerts in order to thrill their audiences. The same is true with Taxi Terry. As you read the story of the cab driver that follows, please remember that if my cabbie didn't have the skill to drive his taxi or didn't possess the knowledge or ability to deliver me to my destination, all the passion in the world would not create a highly engaged customer.

Passion for what you do is a critical element.

However, it is not the only element required for success.

Can you make the effort required to improve at your job? Of course. Can you learn and develop the skills required to improve at your job? Of course.

In fact, the questions for you should be, "*Will you* make the effort required to improve?" and "*Will you* learn and develop the skills?"

If you can answer these questions in the affirmative, you are on your way. You will never be "just an" *anything* ever again.

My experience with Taxi Terry is really an amazing story: and here is a portion of why I have personally found it so surprising. You see, I've been extraordinarily fortunate in my life to encounter many exceptional people. I've met the chairman of General Motors in the boardroom of its Detroit headquarters. At the White House, I was the main speaker for an event that the president of the United States attended. I have had the honor and privilege of addressing the world's finest corporations and their leaders as well as giving speeches for prestigious universities and top business schools.

Yet seven of the most important tenets I have ever observed about business, success, customer service, and creating distinction came from the driver of a cab in which I was riding several years ago.

Certainly, he didn't classify them into seven specific points, and I doubt that he called each one a tenet—which is defined as a belief or principle that you hold as being vitally important even to the point of its being the moral code by which you operate your business or focus your life.

However, everything he did served to display the primary qualities that I find are critically important for every individual—no matter what you do, regardless of where you work—if you want to be better at what you do and grow who you are.

He combined his passion with effort and skill to create distinction in his job and in his life. In addition—and this is a critical aspect—*all* of his elements for greater success and delivering an Ultimate Customer Experience are easily available to you.

It's the story of Taxi Terry.

MY RIDE WITH TAXI TERRY

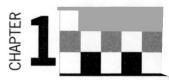

CHAPTER 1

Middle seat, middle of the night.

On one side of me is a guy who could easily pass for the latest parolee from my home state's reformatory. Squeezed into the aisle seat in my row is a man who must be a sumo wrestling champion. Sandwiched between these two strangers, I am doing my best at faking sleep, reading a bit, sipping a Diet Coke, and fighting claustrophobia.

My fellow passengers seem tired and cranky, and so do the flight attendants. Even when the crew members can summon the energy to muster a small semblance of a smile, their eyes are simultaneously sending subversive signals.

"Shark eyes, man, *shark eyes*," the guy in the window seat says to me.

"Uh, what? I'm sorry," I reply, thinking I've missed something. "What did you say?"

"Look at 'er," he orders. "She's cold, man. She has shark eyes. Don't want to cross her; she'd probably throw you off this thing."

"In midair!" Mr. Sumo inserts into the conversation, and then laughs heartily at his own attempt at humor. "She wouldn't give you a drink—or a parachute—on the way out, either!" He guffaws again at his own joke.

How much longer is it to my destination?

I'm occupying space between these two because I'm heading to the northern Florida city of Jacksonville to make a presentation on "the importance of great customer service" to a team of employees at the branch office of a company. However, at this moment I am certainly not on the receiving end of the type of experience I am strongly recommending that every organization deliver to its customers.

We're a couple of hours late, meaning I won't arrive in Jacksonville until a few minutes after midnight, and I'm booked for an early morning breakfast before my speech. I'm already counting the few hours I will be able to sleep, knowing that I have to be at my very best tomorrow for the audience that will be listening to my program: in other words, *my* customers.

It's easy to tell that this is just another segment in a long day of flights for the crew. "Get the cattle—uh, *passengers*—on the plane, shovel a drink and peanuts their way, hope they keep their mouths shut until landing, get them off the plane, then repeat the process" seems to be their way of thinking. However, as we are undoubtedly riding on their last flight of the day, as soon as they can get rid of us, their work will be done. It seems from their demeanor that it cannot happen a moment too soon.

Mr. Sumo evidently swallows a peanut incorrectly and starts to cough. Between hacks, he smiles at the parolee and me and says, "I'm okay . . . just a little too much salt!" Thankful that I will not have to attempt to perform the Heimlich maneuver on this man mountain, I watch as he presses the flight attendant call button.

Slowly approaching the passenger, the cabin attendant stared at him coldly as he asked for a cup of water to relieve his coughing. Acting like a small child, she rolled her eyes to the ceiling, exhaled loudly, and said with a tone of disgust, "Certainly, sir. Just a moment."

About five minutes later, she approached with a cup of water, pushed it in Mr. Sumo's direction, and was gone before he could say, "Thank you."

After what seemed to be an eternity, the captain announced that we were beginning our initial descent into Jacksonville. Since I had been pinned into the middle seat for over an hour, I was hoping my legs would have the blood flow necessary to stand up when we "reached our final destination."

The flight finally got to the runway and gently touched down, the aircraft taxied to the assigned gate, and it was time for me to grab my beat-up carry-on, gather up my tired old body, and head for the terminal.

Exiting the building, I realize that passengers have formed a procession for taxicab pickups. This means that after my long flight, I am going to have a substantial wait to get a ride to the hotel; this is not a pleasant or expected development. I take my place at the end of the line. I surreptitiously determine the number of people in front of me, and my brain becomes like a turnstile, mechanically counting each passenger moving from the line into his or her taxi while I am desperately hoping the queue will move quickly.

Finally, after watching those in front of me get into taxis whisking them to their various destinations, I have arrived at the front of the line. The next cab is *mine*.

Standing there, exhausted and half asleep, I notice out of the corner of my eye that my cab is approaching. The driver halts his vehicle in front of me and then, much to my surprise, springs out of his cab, points his index finger in my direction, and practically shouts at me: "Are *you* ready for the *best* cab ride of your *life*?"

Sheepishly, I look over each shoulder to see if he's speaking to someone else. When I finally realize the comment was directed at me, I shrug and say, "Uh . . . well . . . um . . . yeah. I guess so."

He breaks into a broad smile and says, "Well—*hop on in*!"

Simultaneously, he jogs over to me, grabs my suitcase, and pops open the trunk of his cab as I climb into the backseat. He closes the trunk lid, jumps into the driver's seat, spins around toward me in the back, thrusts out his hand, and inquires, "Mr. McKain?"

Stunned, I respond, "Yes, but *how* did you know my *name*?"

Again he smiles. "Saw it on the name tag on your suitcase. Thought I might as well use it!"

Wiggling his hand a bit to reinforce the idea that he's waiting for a handshake, he states, "I'm *Taxi Terry*."

In my fatigue, all I can think is, "Great. I'm stuck with a *motivational* cab driver."

"Where we heading tonight, Mr. McKain?" he asks.

"The Marriott downtown," I reply.

"Great!" he exclaims. "Let's check out the weather!"

Weather? It hasn't even crossed my mind at midnight what tomorrow's weather is going to be, and frankly, in my tired and grouchy state of mind, I don't even care on this late night in Jacksonville if there is weather. However, when Taxi Terry touches the dashboard of his cab, it seems to light up.

Embedded in the dash in a very elaborate bracket is an old PDA—a pocket PC—with a magnifying glass over the screen; I can clearly read it from the backseat. He has it directed to Weather.com for Jacksonville, and I can clearly observe each second ticking away there on the screen. I now have the "up-to-the-minute" weather forecast for my visit.

"I hope you play golf, Mr. McKain," he says, "because you are going to have a beautiful stay in Jacksonville!"

"Tell me, sir," he continues, seeking to make a more personal connection, "if you don't mind my asking, why are you here?"

"I'm in town to give a speech at the hotel to a group of professionals about customer service," I respond.

"Customer service!" he exclaims. "I am so *into* that!"

I think, "No kidding. It shows." Then he confounds my expectations once again.

He asks, "Would you mind if I record our conversation?" He starts reaching up toward the sun visor. From my spot in the backseat, it appears that he is hitting a button to start recording what we are saying during our ride together into downtown Jacksonville.

Meanwhile, I am thinking, Who *is* this guy?

I have to ask the question. "Wait a second," I say. "Why is your automobile equipped to record conversations—the ones that take place here in your cab?"

"Well, you see, Mr. McKain," he responds, "let's say Dr. Smith—he's a local customer—gets into my cab for a ride to the airport. And during our conversation he mentions that his daughter, Jill, has just enrolled at Vanderbilt

University. As soon as he exits the cab, I hit the button and record that important information."

Taxi Terry isn't done yet, however. "Every night when I return home, I take the information from these recordings I have made and enter it into my database."

I'm thinking, "A *cab driver* . . . with a *database?*" By this point, I knew I was with someone really special.

"Then," Terry continued, "the next time Dr. Smith makes a reservation, this information pops up on my computer. So the doctor gets into the cab, and at some point during our ride to his destination, I will look over and ask him, 'By the way, sir, how is Jill doing at Vanderbilt?'"

He smiles and says, "After that, do you think he will ever ride with anyone else?"

In the darkened backseat of a cab that is approaching downtown Jacksonville, Florida, I shake my head and think to myself, "No. That doctor will never call *anyone else* for a trip to the airport."

During our ride, Taxi Terry educates me on some of his other approaches to the customer experience, but he still has another surprise for me.

In just about every normal cab ride I have experienced on a business trip, upon arrival at the destination, the driver presents the passenger with two forms. Sometimes this information is printed on opposite sides of the same card, and occasionally it is on separate papers. One is a receipt so that the rider can file for expense reimbursement or a tax deduction for the business expense of the transportation, and the second is a business card in hopes the passenger will request the same driver for a return trip once the meeting is near its conclusion.

On this extraordinary trip, however, Taxi Terry pulled in front of the hotel, ran to the trunk of the cab, removed my bag, and held it as if it were a family member. He walked briskly to the hotel employee standing as a sentry at the front door, gently handed the bag to the waiting bellman, and announced he was "presenting Mr. McKain and his luggage!"

It struck me that in my entire life I had never been "presented" to anyone ever before. Taxi Terry had driven me to the Marriott, yet he made me feel like a movie star walking the red carpet at the premiere of a film in which I was the main attraction. That's quite a feat.

Then he turned to me without a card or paper or form in his hand and said, "Mr. McKain, I realize you are going to need a receipt to document the trip for your business purposes, and someone brought you here, so someone is going to have to take you back to the airport, and I hope that's *me*!"

He continued, "You can print your receipt and schedule your return trip on my website"—I'm thinking, "A cab driver . . . with a *website*?"—"at www.TaxiTerry.com!"

However, he still was not finished. "One more thing. Mr. McKain?" he requested. "You mentioned you fly a great deal, which probably means you are riding in a lot of cabs. Well, I'm considering franchising these ideas on how to run a taxi business. So if you ever run into a cab driver who could use some help with customer service"—I am thinking that would probably be all of them—"then you just tell them about Taxi Terry!"

I wanted to give him a standing ovation on the spot. It was a perfect example of an Ultimate Customer Experience.

About This Book

The next morning, as I was preparing for my presentation, I could not get my cab ride and the amazing driver I had met out of my mind. In my profession as a businessperson who delivers speeches to many groups each year, I travel on a constant basis. I'm in a taxi almost every day of my working life. Yet after what must have been literally thousands of experiences as the customer of taxicab companies and their drivers, I realized I had never had an experience like the one Taxi Terry had created for me the previous evening in Jacksonville.

A critical point that I pondered was this: What was it exactly that made the way Taxi Terry did his job so unique for his customer?

It would be easy to say, for example, "He was really friendly." However, lots of other cabbies had been friendly, yet none had left the impression that Taxi Terry did on me.

I could say that his service was superior—and it was in a manner of speaking—yet ultimately he did exactly what his competition would have done. He took me from the airport to the Marriott safely and in a timely manner. Whether I was in the back of a long, shiny limousine or in Taxi Terry's cab, that outcome would have been the same. So why did I not even consider riding back to the airport with anyone other than Terry? I've ridden in nicer cars that served as cabs, and sometimes the groups having me speak will even send a driver wearing a uniform in a black town car for transportation. Nothing, however, made the impression that Taxi Terry did.

I sat down and examined each part of the ride I'd had on the previous evening with Terry and realized that there were seven critical factors that made it extraordinary. In this book, we'll examine each of those points—calling them tenets—discover why they are so important, and provide basic ideas on how you can deliver them in your work so that you can become a Taxi Terry to the people with whom you work and the customers whom you serve.

Let's get started with the first tenet!

Taxi Terry Takeaway

Obviously, Taxi Terry provided an extraordinary experience; however, the inbound flight to Jacksonville created an experience for the airline's customers as well.

- What are three aspects of the manner in which the flight attendants treated their customers on the plane that created an inferior experience for those passengers?

- Do you or your organization inadvertently deliver some of those approaches when you are speaking with your customers?

- If so, how can you change that, starting right now?

THE FIRST TENET

Set High Expectations and Then Exceed Them.

CHAPTER **2**

What do you expect when the phone rings?

Your answer, I would be very willing to wager, depends on at least two variables:

1. The time of day when it rings

2. Your situation as it rings

Imagine that you've just sat down to dinner at the customary hour and the phone begins to ring; as you note from the caller ID, the incoming call is from a number you don't recognize. Quite possibly, you begin to immediately become irritated. You strongly suspect that another bothersome call from a script-reading, impersonal telemarketing agent is about to commence.

However, if you insisted that your son return home by midnight and the phone rings at 11:55 p.m., you are undoubtedly anticipating some kind of lame excuse for his being late. Or perhaps you are prepared to listen to a "sales presentation" of sorts from your son on why he should be allowed another hour with his friends instead of being the only kid in the entire school who has to be home by 12.

Let's say you've had some unexpected and unavoidable expenses and your mortgage is unusually late. When the phone rings, you may feel your stomach get a bit queasy. You may expect that someone from the bank is on the other end of the line, wondering when you are going to round up the money to make the required payment.

Or maybe you're in a new romance. The phone rings first thing in the morning, and you feel your heart flutter, anticipating that your new love is calling to wish you a good morning and discuss plans for the coming evening.

Before Androids and iPhones and programmable ringtones based on the identity of the caller, every time the telephone rang, it sounded exactly the same regardless of who was making the call. The ring from the mortgage company or the late teenager sounded no different from that of the new love or the telemarketer. Therefore, it had to be something other than the actual telephone ring that made you feel the way you did at the moment of the call.

Obviously, the critical difference was the *expectations* you had about what was about to occur. Positive expectations could make your heart skip a beat; negative expectations might mean nausea. Nonetheless, the expectation of what was about to transpire created a significant—and very real—response that was both physical and emotional. You did not experience those emotions because of what had happened—the ringing of the phone—instead, your feelings were predicated on what you predicted would happen next.

These examples are meant to prove that what you expected to occur generated a feeling within you regarding your anticipation of expected outcomes and that those expectations affected the results.

If the telemarketer's call surprises you and you aren't mentally or emotionally prepared to deal with the pressure tactics, you may find yourself listening to the pitch for much longer than you would have if you had steeled yourself in advance for the sales presentation. In fact, you might even surprise yourself and purchase what they have to offer.

However, if you correctly anticipate that it is a telemarketer causing your telephone to ring near the dinner hour, not only are you prepared to refuse the